Dave's Big Day

Contents

Written by
Emma Lynch

Sunday 8 May.
My mate Dave is eight today.

Dave wakes up.

"Hey, Dave," says his dad.

"It's the big day today! Hooray!"

Presents

Wow! Thank you!

Dave has his presents.
He gets some skates and a model railway.

stunt plane

18th May
Stunt
Display

Dave gets a trip to a **stunt plane** display.

Cake

eggs

butter

scales

Mr Rein makes a cake. He weighs the butter on the **scales**.

Then he adds eggs.
Next, he bakes the cake.

Dave's mates

Dave's mates come to play.
"Hi, Mrs Rein. Hi, Mr Rein. Hi, Dave,"
they say.

Jake brings Dave a snake.
Freya brings him some crayons.

No way! That's wicked!

Dave

Jay brings Dave a train for his railway.

Dave and his mates play fun games.

Lunch

Midday. Now for lunch!
There are milkshakes to drink.
There are plates and plates of food.

There are cupcakes and pancakes.
There are raisins and grapes.

Hip, hip, hooray!

Mr Rein brings Dave his cake.

The cake is in the shape of an eight!
Hip, hip, hooray for Dave!

scales   tells you how much something weighs

stunt plane   a plane that can turn cartwheels in the air!